Nature's Children

RHINOCEROS

Merebeth Switzer

GROLIER
EDUCATIONAL

PH

FACTS IN BRIEF

Classification of Rhinoceros

Class: *Mammalia* (mammals)

Order: *Perissodactyla* (odd-toed ungulates)

Family: *Rhinocerotidae* (rhinoceros family)

Genera: *Ceratotherium, Diceros, Dicerorhinus, Rhinoceros.*

Species: *Diceros bicornis* (Black Rhinoceros);
Ceratotherium simum (White Rhinoceros);
Dicerorhinus sumatrensis (Sumatran Rhinoceros);
Rhinoceros unicornis (Indian Rhinoceros);
Rhinoceros sondaicus (Javan Rhinoceros).

World distribution. Parts of Africa and Asia.

Habitat. Varies with species.

Distinctive physical characteristics. Rhinoceroses are large animals with thick skin, one or two horns in the middle of the head and three-toed feet.

Habits. Vary with species.

Diet. Vegetation.

Published originally as
"Getting to Know . . . Nature's Children."

This series is approved and recommended by the Federation of Ontario Naturalists.

This library reinforced edition is available exclusively from:

GROLIER
EDUCATIONAL

Sherman Turnpike, Danbury, Connecticut 06816

Contents

It is a hot, dusty day on the African plain. Herds of zebras and antelopes gather around a waterhole, and a secretary bird struts along the edge of the pool. Several pairs of hippo eyes and hippo ears peek out of the water.

A snorting, puffing sound is heard from the nearby bushes and out into the clearing trots a huge White Rhinoceros. It wades noisily into the water, then SPLASH! Rolling around, the rhino covers itself with a thick coat of mud to keep it cool in the hot African sun.

But not all rhinos live in Africa or on hot dusty plains. If you'd like to find out more about these huge animals and how they live, keep reading.

A Big Little Baby

When a rhino baby is born, it looks very tiny compared to its mother. Nonetheless, it weighs up to twenty times as much as an average human baby—and it is not nearly as helpless. In fact, within hours it is up on its feet and taking its first unsteady steps.

By the time it is a couple of weeks old, the young rhino will be playing tag and wrestling with other babies, charging at its mom for fun or trying to sneak up on her from behind. Already it is learning skills that it will need when it's older.

Sticking close to mom.

Rhino Relatives

There are five types of rhinos. The largest one, the White Rhinoceros, lives on the plains of southern and northeastern Africa. Its closest relative, the Black Rhinoceros, also lives in Africa, anywhere from the dense rain forests to dry scrublands. The smallest of all the rhinos is the Sumatran Rhinoceros, and it's found in the southeast Asian countries of Sumatra, Malaya, Thailand and Burma. The Indian Rhinoceros lives on protected game reserves in Assam, West Bengal and Nepal, while the Javan Rhinoceros can only be found on a game reserve in Java in southeast Asia.

Scientists think rhinos' closest relatives are the elephant and the hippopotamus.

The Sumatran rhino is so timid that it is seldom seen.

Leave Me Alone!

Most rhinos like to live alone, except, of course, for a mom and her baby. Males usually remain completely on their own except when it's time to mate.

White rhinos, however, are a little more sociable. They live in groups of up to 18, including a male, several females and a number of babies, or calves. Indian rhinos will sometimes also live in small groups.

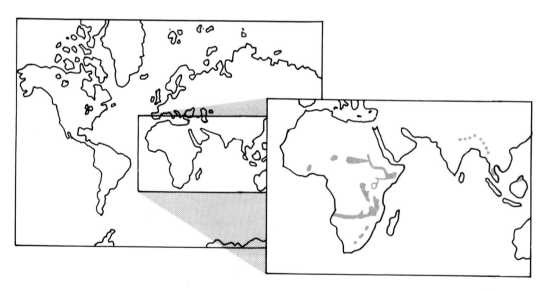

The colored areas on this map show where rhinoceroses live.

Home Sweet Home

Female rhinos live on territories ranging in size from 3 to 15 square kilometres (1.2 to 5.8 square miles) or even more when food or water is hard to find. One female's territory can overlap with another's and they don't usually defend the borders of their range. White rhino females often meet each other with nose-to-nose greetings, but Indian rhinos tend to be less friendly.

Males' territories are generally smaller than those of the females, up to about 4 square kilometres (1.5 square miles). However, most males mark the boundaries of their home range with their droppings and defend their territories fiercely against other males.

The Black rhino has a reputation for being bad tempered.

Big, Bigger, Biggest

You already know that the White rhino is the biggest rhino, but did you know that the only land animal that's bigger is the elephant? The White rhino is taller than most adult men and can weigh up to 3600 kilograms (8000 pounds). That's more than three small cars!

The Sumatran rhino is the smallest. It weighs only a little more than one small car and it probably isn't much taller than you. All the other rhinos are in between these two in height and weight. Females are usually the same size as the males or a little smaller.

Despite its size, the White rhino is peaceful and tends to run from trouble rather than charge.

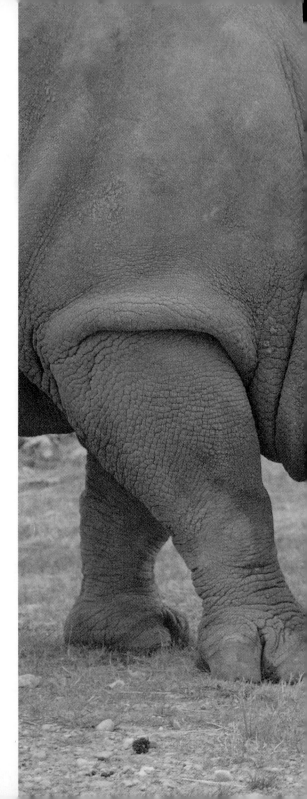

Horned Giants

All rhinos have at least one horn
—even calves are born with tiny
ones. In fact, the name
rhinoceros means "horn-nosed."
Indian and Javan rhinos have
only one horn, while both of the
African rhinos and the Sumatran
rhino have two. The two horns sit
in a row up the middle of the
rhino's snout, with the largest one
always in front.

The Black and White rhinos
have the biggest horns, and we do
mean BIG. The front horn of the
Black rhino is about as long as
your arm! Both these African
rhinos use their horns to defend
themselves.

*The rhino uses its horn to protect
itself or to help win the battle for
a mate.*

16

Hairy Horn

It's difficult to believe that something as hard as a rhino's horn is made of the same material as your hair, but it's true. The material is called keratin and is formed by the clumping together of hair-like fibers. Your fingernails and toenails are made of keratin too.

The rhino's horn may look like a cow's or sheep's, but unlike those animals' horns, which scientists call *true* horns, it has no bone in the middle.

Because a rhino's horn has no bony core, there's hardly any bleeding if it's broken off in a fight and soon a new horn begins to grow.

If you get this close to a rhino's horn, you're too close!

Sound Scoops and Super Sniffers

Rhinos are so short-sighted that they can't tell a person from a small tree at a distance of more than 30 metres (100 feet). And since the rhino's tiny eyes are over on the sides of its head, the rhino must turn its head to see anything in front of it.

But the rhino makes up for its poor eyesight with its excellent hearing and its superkeen sense of smell. A rhino's ears can swivel around so that they act like little "sound scoops" to pick up the slightest of sounds. And as for smell, the rhino's huge snout is filled with chambers that gather messages about the aromas drifting around.

A nose for trouble.

A Suit of Armor

Does the gray skin of this Indian rhino remind you of a suit of armor? Those large skin folds make it look like it's covered in overlapping plates that could almost be metal. These folds help scientists tell the difference between the types of rhinos. Both the Indian and Javan rhino have a skin fold at the base of the tail, but only the Javan rhino has a complete fold of skin like a collar around its neck.

The Sumatran rhino is easy to tell from its Asian cousins because it has long hairs scattered over its body. All other rhinos, including the African White and Black rhinos, lose their hair as they grow up, until they're left with just ear and tail tufts—and, of course, eyelashes! A rhino uses its tail to swish away flies.

Meals and Mouths

Rhinos are plant eaters and they crunch down huge amounts of greens every day. Some rhinos graze on grass, while others browse on small shrubs, trees and leaves. Some feed on both and a few even eat fresh fruit. What a rhino eats depends on the shape of its mouth and lips.

White rhinos like to eat short grasses. Their wide, flat mouth and broad lips help them take big bites while feeding. These rhinos also have a hard ridge in their mouths to cut the grass stalks. The White rhino is the only one with a square snout, and some people think its name actually comes from the misinterpretation of a word meaning "wide" that described its broad mouth.

The Black rhino eats some grass but it feeds mostly on small shrubs and trees. Its tapered upper lip can grasp like a hand to tear twigs and leaves. The other rhinos also have skilled, rather pointy lips that can grasp branches and leaves and even pluck small fruit. The Indian rhino can also fold its upper lip to one side to make grazing on short grass easier.

Opposite page:
Given its size, it's no wonder a rhino eats huge amounts of food each day.

Grinders and Jabbers

You might think that with all those plants to eat, rhinos would need lots of teeth. Actually, they only need large molars to grind down the grasses and twigs. In fact, neither the Black nor the White rhino has front teeth at all!

The Asian rhinos do have front teeth, called incisors, but they use them mainly as weapons. Instead of relying on their horn to protect themselves, they attack their enemies by jabbing them with their lower front teeth.

"Look, kids, no cavities!"

Getting Around

Despite their short, thick legs, rhinos are surprisingly speedy. They can gallop as fast as 40 kilometres (25 miles) an hour, and a charging rhino can accelerate faster than a truck. And they can even change direction quickly.

All rhinos like to wallow in mudholes or shallow water, but they are also good swimmers. The Indian rhino is considered the champ—it can cross wide rivers and is a very good diver—and there have been reports of Sumatran rhinos swimming in the sea.

The rhino has a quite springy gait for such a heavy animal.

Club Tracks

It's easy to pick out a rhino's tracks from those of any other animal. All rhinos have three toes on each foot, a wide one in the middle with a smaller one to each side. As a result, a rhino's footprint looks like the ace of clubs from a deck of playing cards.

Each toe is tipped with a wide, blunt nail.

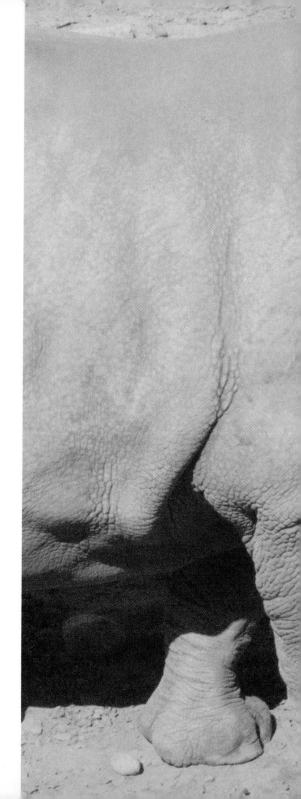

Happy Together

When you see rhinos in the wild, you'll rarely see them without little birds walking over them and picking at their skin. These small birds are oxpeckers and they've worked out a special relationship with rhinos and other animals.

In return for a free ride and all the insects they can eat, the oxpeckers keep the rhino healthy by removing pesky parasites. Along with cattle egrets, they also eat any insects the rhinos stir up as they walk.

Note the oxpeckers on these rhinos. They will even poke into their hosts' ears looking for a free meal.

Marvelous Mud

Rhinos spend a lot of time at waterholes. Indian rhinos like to lie in the water but African rhinos prefer to roll in the mud at the edge of the pool. They make giant mud puddles called wallows and roll in them until they're covered in a thick coat of mud.

Even though rhinos have thick skin, the outer layer is thin and has many blood vessels and nerves just below it. Insect bites and sunburn are very irritating to a rhino. A good coating of mud both keeps away biting flies and protects rhinos from the heat.

Nothing like a cooling coat of mud!

Daytime, Nighttime

Rhinos may be active at night or in the day,
depending on where they live. Those that live on
the hot, dry plains rest most of the day under a
shady tree or in a cool mudhole. They only begin
to feed in the late afternoon and often spend
their nights grazing or playing and chasing each
other at a waterhole.

Rhinos that live in cooler rain forests can be
more active during the day, but even they will
likely interrupt their wanderings now and then
for a short nap.

Taking it easy.

Mating Time

Although rhinos tend to live alone, they do get together when it's time to mate. Often the female, or cow, will journey quite far in search of a male. As she travels through different males' territories, she gives off a scent that tells the males, called bulls, that she is ready to mate.

If more than one bull picks up her scent, there may be thunderous, head-bashing battles. Even the cow and bull may charge and battle with each other!

After mating, the bull sometimes remains with the female for a short time, but usually they separate and the female is left to care for her baby alone.

A pair of heavyweights.

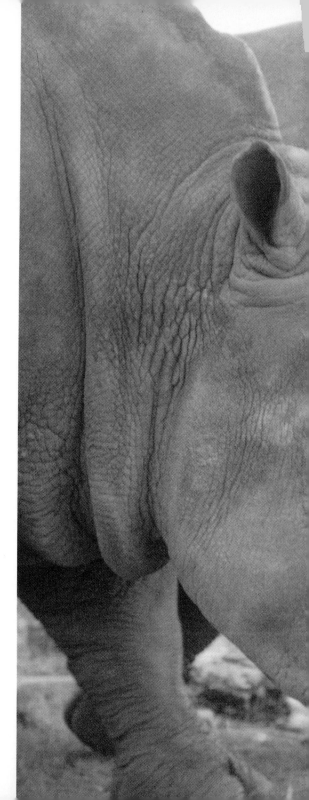

Welcome to the World

Fourteen to eighteen months after mating, the mother rhino gives birth. Almost always she has just one baby, but occasionally there are twins.

Just a couple of days after it is born, the baby is trotting along with its mother as she searches for food and water. The calf nurses from its mother and needs what would amount to about 100 glasses of milk each day! Within a few weeks of its birth, the baby is also eating grass or twigs.

The rhino is a very good mother.

Growing Up

A baby rhino stays close to its mom and nurses from her for about a year. She protects it from enemies such as lions, hyenas and crocodiles until it is big enough to protect itself. If there is a group of rhinos, they may form a defensive circle, backing together around any babies and facing outward. Few enemies are brave—or foolish—enough to tackle a wall of dangerous horns.

A calf will stay with its mom until it is about three years old, then it will find its own group or territory. By the time it's five to eight years old, it is ready to start its own family.

Following in mom's footsteps.

Rhino Alert

Rhinoceroses have been around for a very long time. Their ancestors, some of which had as many as five horns on their heads, roamed the earth millions of years ago. Today, five species remain, but the question is, for how long? Rhinos are among the rarest animals in the world. Scientists think there are less than 20 000 living wild, and they fear there are only 65 Javan rhinos left.

One reason rhinos are so endangered is that they are hunted for their horns, which some people mistakenly think can be ground and used as medicine.

There is hope for the rhinos, however. They are now protected by law, and reserves have been established. Their numbers are slowly increasing, and with some luck and enough care rhinos will be spending their days charging through forests or happily wallowing in mudholes for a long time to come.

Words to Know

Bull   A male rhinoceros.

Calf   A young rhinoceros.

Cow   A female rhinoceros.

Incisors   Sharp teeth near the front of the mouth.

Keratin   The material that a rhino's horn is made of, as are
   fingernails and hair.

Mammal   Any warm-blooded animal that gives birth to live
   young and produces milk for them.

Mate   To come together to produce young. Either member of an
   animal pair is also the other's mate.

Molars   Large blunt teeth that are used for grinding.

Oxpeckers   Small African birds that feed on the parasites on the
   hides of rhinoceroses.

Reserve   An area where wildlife is protected by law.

Territory   An area that an animal or group of animals lives in,
   and usually defends from animals of the same kind.

Wallow   A mudpatch a rhinoceros makes to lie in.

INDEX

Cover Photo: Bill Ivy

Photo Credits: E.R. Degginger, pages 4, 12, 37, 42; Gerald & Buff Corsi, page 7; World Wildlife Federation, page 8; Keith Gunnar (The Stock Market Inc.), page 11; Bill Ivy, pages 15, 16, 19, 23, 26, 27, 33, 38, 41; Boyd Norton, page 20; Joseph A. DiChello, Jr., page 24; Jim Cronk, page 29; G.C. Kelley, page 30; Suzanne L. Murphy, page 34; W. Smyth, page 45.